AF207019

BECOME AN
AUTO MECHANIC

by Ib Larsen

BrightPoint Press

San Diego, CA

© 2025 BrightPoint Press
an imprint of ReferencePoint Press, Inc.
Printed in the United States

For more information, contact:
BrightPoint Press
PO Box 27779
San Diego, CA 92198
www.BrightPointPress.com

LIBRARY OF CONGRESS CATALOGING-IN-PUBLICATION DATA

Names: Larsen, Ib, author.
Title: Become an auto mechanic / by Ib Larsen.
Description: San Diego, CA: BrightPoint Press, [2025] | Series: Skilled and vocational trades | Includes bibliographical references and index. | Audience: Grades 7–9
Identifiers: LCCN 2024001070 (print) | LCCN 2024001071 (eBook) | ISBN 9781678209544 (hardcover) | ISBN 9781678209551 (eBook)
Subjects: LCSH: Automobiles--Maintenance and repair--Vocational guidance--Juvenile literature. | Automobile mechanics--Juvenile literature.
Classification: LCC TL152.L277 2025 (print) | LCC TL152 (eBook) | DDC 629.28/7023--dc23/eng/20240128
LC record available at https://lccn.loc.gov/2024001070
LC eBook record available at https://lccn.loc.gov/2024001071

CONTENTS

AT A GLANCE

- Auto mechanics maintain cars and repair them when they break down.

- Auto mechanics work at auto service shops, auto repair shops, and car dealerships.

- Being an auto mechanic is a trade job. This is a job that requires advanced training but no degree.

- Most employers require auto mechanics to have a high school diploma or a General Educational Development (GED) degree.

- Auto mechanics can be trained as apprentices. Apprentices work alongside experienced mechanics.

- Auto mechanics need to follow safety procedures to avoid danger.

- Auto mechanics usually work regular daytime hours. Sometimes they work overtime in the evenings or on weekends.

- Car technology is always changing. Auto mechanics have to keep learning in order to work on the newest cars.

- In 2022, about 12 percent of auto mechanics were women. That portion has been slowly growing over the years.

WHY BECOME AN AUTO MECHANIC?

Alex Koontz never knows what to expect when he goes into work. He is an auto mechanic. A typical morning may begin with a simple oil change. Or he might spend all day figuring out a problem with a car's computer system. Alex loves the variety of his job.

Alex has liked cars since high school. In his junior year, he took an automotive class. The next year, he entered a

Auto mechanics like to solve problems. They may spend most of the day trying to fix an issue on one car.

mechanic competition. He got second place. That earned him a scholarship to study car repair at a local college. He began his career as an apprentice. That means he worked under an experienced mechanic.

Auto mechanics do everything from fixing brakes to changing the oil and other fluids in a car.

He learned a lot and soon became an auto mechanic himself.

Alex works at a car dealership in Newport Beach, California. He works on expensive Jaguar and Land Rover cars. He even drives a Jaguar himself. And he's only 20 years old. Alex's success has pleased his parents. His father said, "I am very proud that Alex went the technical route, to work on cars."[1] Being an auto mechanic is something to be proud of.

WHAT IS AN AUTO MECHANIC?

Auto mechanics like Alex fix cars. They are people who like cars. They also like to work with their hands. There are many ways to train as an auto mechanic. But no matter how they train, auto mechanics become

Car dealerships and repair shops have lifts that allow
mechanics to easily work under cars.

experts at fixing vehicles. They help people keep their cars running smoothly.

Many people in the United States own cars. In 2021, 91.7 percent of US households had at least one vehicle. People rely on their cars to get to work, school, and more. And when something goes wrong with their cars, they rely on auto mechanics.

CHAPTER ONE

WHAT DOES AN AUTO MECHANIC DO?

Auto mechanics repair and maintain cars. They work on many different makes and models of cars. The make of a car is the brand that produces it. The model of a car is the specific kind of car it is. For example, the Ford Focus is a popular car in the United States. Its make is Ford, and its model is the Focus. Cars need regular care to make sure they keep working. This can mean changing a car's oil or replacing

Mechanics change air filters during routine car maintenance, such as oil changes.

its **air filter**. Auto mechanics also repair damaged cars. Cars can get damaged in accidents. Or they can break down over time. Auto mechanics fix cars to get them back on the road.

Modern cars are complex machines. People may not be able to fix their own cars. Auto mechanics are trained to spot problems with a car. They look for loose or broken parts. They listen for unusual noises, such as grinding or whistling. They use **diagnostic** strategies to narrow down the problem. If a vehicle needs work, an auto mechanic can do it.

When a car needs repairs, its owner can take it to an auto mechanic. Mechanics will inspect the car. They will give the owner an estimate of how much the repairs will cost.

Then, the mechanics will fix or replace the parts that are damaged. For example, a car that has had a rear-end crash may need a new back bumper.

Sometimes mechanics use computers to run diagnostic tests to figure out a problem.

Many mechanics work at chain repair shops such as Midas. Chain shops have locations all over the country.

WHERE DO AUTO MECHANICS WORK?

Auto mechanics often work at auto repair shops. These garages have the tools and space that mechanics need to work on vehicles. Auto mechanics also work at car dealerships. These are places that buy and sell new and used cars. Mechanics also work at tire stores and auto parts shops.

Some auto repair shops are large national chains. These shops employ lots of auto mechanics in the United States. Chains include Midas, Meineke Car Care Centers, and AAMCO. Auto mechanics can also start their own auto repair shops. Owning a business gives a mechanic more control over how things are done. But running a business can be hard. Business owners have to make the right decisions in order to earn money.

Auto collision centers employ auto mechanics as well. These places are also known as body shops. This is because they work on the outside parts of cars. Cars that have been in accidents might need new bumpers, windows, or mirrors. They may also have dents and scratched paint.

Mechanics at body shops can fix these issues.

Some auto repair shops work on only certain kinds of cars. These are called specialty shops. Mechanics at these shops have special skills. For example, a shop might specialize in Toyota cars. This repair shop will employ mechanics who know a lot about Toyotas.

TEAMWORK

Auto mechanics can work alone or in teams. At some shops, every mechanic can handle most jobs that come in. At other shops, each mechanic has a specific role. For instance, a mechanic might work only on transmission systems. These are the parts in a car that send power from the engine to the wheels. These systems are complex, so mechanics specialize in fixing them.

Some jobs can be performed alone. Other jobs may require more than one person. For example, two people are

Mechanics sometimes work together to fix different parts of a car.

required to work on the **hydraulics** in a brake system. This is because different parts of the car need to be worked on at the same time. Heavy lifting sometimes requires extra pairs of hands. But lifting machines and car jacks can help a single mechanic work alone.

Teamwork skills can help a mechanic get a job. Dustin Peugeot is the founder of a trade institute for auto technicians.

Types of Car Lifts

A car lift is a machine that lifts cars off the ground. This allows auto mechanics to work underneath the car. There are four main types of car lifts. These are in-ground lifts, two-post lifts, four-post lifts, and scissor lifts. Auto mechanics use different lifts for different jobs.

Mechanics must remove a car's wheels to check the brakes.

He explains, "Being able to show that you're a team player will work to your advantage when it comes time to find a job. When hiring auto mechanics, employers want to make sure you'll be a good fit for the shop."[2]

CHAPTER TWO

WHAT TRAINING DO AUTO MECHANICS NEED?

There are many ways to become an auto mechanic. Some people work under experts as apprentices. Other people attend **vocational colleges**. There, they earn degrees in automotive technology. But the first step is to get a high school diploma. Most employers require their mechanics to have one. People who do not graduate from high school can get a GED certification. A GED can stand in for a high school degree.

Many auto mechanics complete hours of hands-on training under the guidance of the staff at an auto repair shop.

PARTS OF A CAR

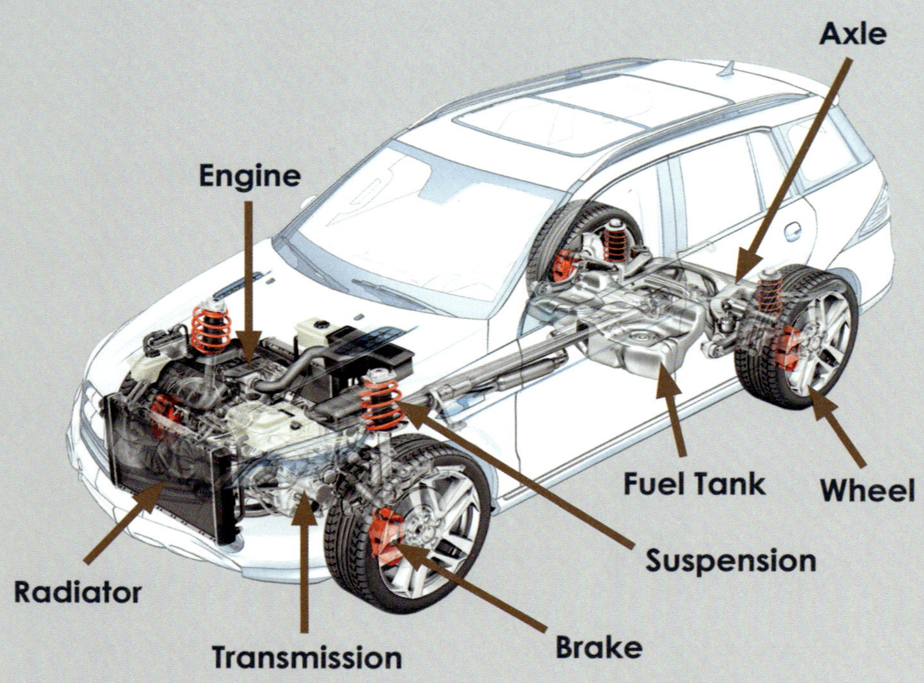

This diagram identifies the main parts of a car with an internal combustion engine that auto mechanics typically repair.

There are ways high school students can prepare to become auto mechanics. They might **shadow** a mechanic on the job. This allows the students to spend time with an auto mechanic. They can learn what mechanics do and see exactly what the job is like. High school senior Bailey McCartney spent a few days shadowing a mechanic. This mechanic worked on school buses. "You get to be here with someone who has done this for years, and you get to figure out if this is something that you really want to do,"[3] she explained. Students can also take classes that teach them the skills mechanics use. These courses include shop classes and math classes.

EDUCATION

A bachelor's degree is not necessary to become an auto mechanic. But some people earn vocational degrees before applying for mechanic jobs. Vocational schools prepare students to do specific trade jobs. These programs typically

take 2 years to complete. At the end
of their education, students graduate
with a vocational degree. People can
get vocational degrees in many different
subjects. These include construction,
welding, and plumbing. To become an
auto mechanic, students earn degrees in
automotive technology.

Vocational students learn from teachers
in classrooms. But they also apply what
they have learned in hands-on activities.
For example, an automotive technology
student may change a car's oil. Daytime
students typically attend classes for 8 hours
a day. But some schools offer night classes
for students who work during the day.
Anoka Technical College offers a program
to become an automotive technician.

Students in the program take classes including Vehicle Electronics and General Auto Service.

Many people choose to get vocational degrees before becoming an auto mechanic. By earning a degree, students learn a lot about the job. Employers prefer

Some automotive classrooms have car parts that students can study during classroom time.

people who have experience working with cars. Having a vocational degree improves a student's chance of being hired. Many vocational schools advertise how likely their graduates are to get a job. The Automotive Technician program at Anoka has a job placement rate of more than 90 percent.

APPRENTICESHIPS

Another way to train as an auto mechanic is to be an apprentice. This is someone who works under an experienced professional. Many trades offer apprenticeships. Apprentices usually work full time and get paid. As they work, they learn how to do the job. Eventually, they can become lead auto mechanics. Apprenticeships usually take a year or more to complete.

Becoming an apprentice is a good way to get on-the-job experience. One mechanic explained that he learned a lot from the older mechanics at his shop. He said, "They gave me helpful hints and shortcuts that made diagnosis and repair much easier."[4] Learning from experts as an apprentice is a great way to become an auto mechanic.

CERTIFICATIONS

There is a lot to learn to become an auto mechanic. But the learning doesn't stop once a mechanic gets a job. Even experienced mechanics earn certifications. These are documents that prove a person is trained in specific tasks. Auto mechanics

Apprenticeships give beginning mechanics a chance to learn directly from experts in the automotive field.

Auto mechanics must demonstrate that they can successfully complete many different car maintenance tasks to become a master technician.

can earn their Automotive Service

Excellence (ASE) certification.

There are 58 ASE certification tests.

Each has to do with a different part of

being an auto mechanic. These tests
cover automotive subjects such as engine
repair. Earning an ASE certification shows
that a mechanic knows a skill. This means
employers prefer auto mechanics with
ASE certifications. Some employers
even require their employees to have
certain certifications.

Become a Master Technician

Auto mechanics can earn ASE certifications
in a series of related tests. By doing this, they
can become master technicians. For example,
becoming a master automobile technician
requires passing eight tests. This takes a lot of
time and energy. But mechanics who pass the
tests become masters of their trade.

CHAPTER THREE

WHAT IS LIFE LIKE AS AN AUTO MECHANIC?

ost auto mechanics are employed full time. That means they work around 40 hours a week, or 8 hours a day. They usually work 6- to 12-hour shifts each day.

The Bureau of Labor Statistics (BLS) states that overtime among auto mechanics is common. When a lot of cars need repairs, mechanics work evenings and weekends. One mechanic might need to work on ten cars in a single day.

Before they begin work, mechanics discuss with customers what needs to be fixed on a car.

A DAY'S WORK

A typical day for auto mechanics depends on where they work. It also depends on what their personal skills and duties are. Some shops offer only car maintenance. The mechanics working there will perform only those services. Body shops focus mainly on repairing the outsides of damaged vehicles. They typically won't fix problems inside cars. That's a job for mechanics at an auto repair shop. These mechanics work on parts such as the engine.

Before mechanics work on a car, they talk to the owner. This is the auto mechanic's chance to ask questions about the car. They will ask what issues the owner is having with the car. They might ask if the car has been making unusual sounds or vibrations. And they might also want to know if it has needed repairs before. The mechanic will then figure out the problem with the car. They will let the car owner know what work needs to be done. And they will give the owner an estimate of

When the outside of a car is damaged, mechanics who work at a body shop can fix it.

One of the most common car maintenance tasks a
mechanic performs is an oil change.

the cost. The owner can then give the
mechanic permission to begin working on
the car.

Different jobs take different amounts of
time. An oil change usually takes less than
an hour. Replacing the transmission system
could take days. Once the job is done, the
car owner picks up the car. This is usually
when the car owner pays the mechanic.

SKILLS AND TOOLS

Auto mechanics may have to talk to a
lot of customers. They need to listen to
what customers say about their cars. And
they have to explain car issues in a way
customers will understand. This means it
is important for mechanics to have good
communication skills. Auto mechanics also

need to be able to solve problems. They must know a lot about cars to be able to fix them. Finally, auto mechanics must like working with their hands. They use lots of tools in a typical day. Some tools require strength and care. For many mechanics, this is the best part of the job. Mechanic Drake Davis says, "I came into this **industry** because I love working with my hands and trying to diagnose and repair each problem."[5]

Auto mechanics use dozens of tools to work on cars. They usually bring their own small tools to work. These include hammers, pliers, screwdrivers, and wrenches. Auto mechanics organize their tools in a toolbox. Other tools are large and expensive. These include machines such as

Mechanics use many tools to work on cars. These tools help them fix cars and remove parts to reach what needs fixing.

car lifts. These tools are usually provided by the shop the mechanic works for.

STAYING SAFE

Being an auto mechanic can be dangerous. Mechanics must follow safety rules to avoid injury. The company an auto mechanic works for should follow clear safety standards.

One risk auto mechanics face is injuries from heavy lifting. Lifting improperly can injure a mechanic's back. Mechanics need to be trained to lift things safely. Another risk for mechanics is exposure to loud noise. Tools such as electric drills can be very loud, especially in a garage. To avoid hearing loss, mechanics wear earmuffs or foam earplugs. One more risk is exposure to harmful chemicals. These include gasoline, paint thinner, and **solvents**. It's important for mechanics to handle and

Mechanics use drills for many tasks, including removing wheels.

Mechanics must be careful when working with dangerous chemicals.

store these chemicals properly. That means following the directions printed on the containers of chemicals.

Mechanics who follow safety rules on the job can enjoy their careers without worrying about injury. For those who love cars, being an auto mechanic can be a fun and interesting job. No two days are the same. Auto technician Faye Hadley explains, "I never know what to expect because every day, every project, brings me something different."[6] Plus, car technology is always changing. Auto mechanics have a lot to look forward to in the future of their profession.

Safety Statistics

Safety is important. The Bureau of Labor Statistics keeps track of workplace injuries and deaths. Injuries to the hands and back are the most common for auto mechanics. Following safety procedures can keep mechanics safe from injury.

CHAPTER FOUR

WHAT IS THE FUTURE FOR AUTO MECHANICS?

In 2022, the BLS estimated that there were 782,200 auto mechanic jobs in the United States. It expected that by 2032, there will be 12,800 more auto mechanic jobs. But some have argued that this is not enough. The website *MarketWatch* reported that enrollment in automotive educational programs dropped between 2020 and 2022. It fell by 20 percent. But around the same time, demand for auto mechanics

More auto mechanics are needed to maintain older cars, which usually need more repairs.

was on the rise. There are several reasons for this increase. One is that cars are lasting longer. Older cars need more frequent visits to auto mechanics. Another is that new car technology requires auto mechanics to have more education. But fewer people are graduating from the vocational programs that give auto mechanics that education.

An auto mechanic's pay depends on several factors. These include education,

Auto Mechanic Pay by State

The District of Columbia has the highest pay for auto mechanics. The state with the highest average pay for auto mechanics is Alaska. Auto mechanics in Alaska made an average of $60,640 a year in 2022. The next three highest-paying states for auto mechanics in 2022 were California, Washington, and New Jersey.

experience, and location. An auto mechanic with a vocational degree is likely to earn more than a mechanic without a degree. The BLS reported that the median auto mechanic salary in 2022 was $46,970. Some mechanics are paid hourly for their work. Others are paid according to how many cars they work on.

NEW TECHNOLOGY

Cars are always changing. They are getting safer and more **fuel efficient**. And car companies are always adding new features to their cars. To keep up, mechanics must study these new technologies.

Cars have had computer-controlled systems for a long time. The first car to have a computer was produced in 1968.

This computer controlled the fuel system. But since the 1990s, cars have relied more and more on computers. In modern cars, computers can control the engine, the braking system, and the safety features. Auto mechanics need to know how to work on a car's computer. A diagnostic tool makes this job easier. A car's computer can sometimes detect a problem. The mechanic plugs a diagnostic tool into the car's computer. The tool might be able to read what the problem is.

Another new technology that is changing the lives of auto mechanics is electric vehicles (EVs). A gas-powered engine uses gasoline for fuel. Burning this fuel creates force that is used to turn the car's wheels. But in an EV, a motor powered by electricity

turns the wheels directly. Working on an
EV is a lot different from working on a gas
vehicle. Mechanics have to know more
about computers. And although both EVs
and gas cars have batteries, their batteries
work differently. At the same time, EVs

**Modern cars have many computer systems, which
require special tools to fix.**

As more people buy EVs, mechanics are undergoing training to learn how to fix the cars' computer systems and batteries.

have fewer moving parts than gas vehicles. This means that EVs require less regular maintenance than gas cars. More and more EVs are sold every year. As EVs become

more common, auto mechanics will have to
learn how to work on them.

SUPPORTING THE NEXT GENERATION

Becoming an auto mechanic means
learning from those with experience in
the field. Apprentices learn from their
mentors. Students at vocational schools
learn from their teachers. Experts pass
what they know to the next generation of
auto mechanics.

The Youth Automotive Training
Center (YATC) is a program in Deerfield
Beach, Florida. It gives 16- through
21-year-olds a free 9-month education in
automotive technology. Jeremy Ross Jr.
graduated from YATC in 2020. He dreamed

Students learn how to fix different parts of cars in hands-on vocational auto mechanics classes.

of owning a business where he could work on cars. He said, "At YATC, they help you out a lot. The people here guide you in the right direction."[7] His mentors taught him how to work on cars. They got him started on his dream.

WOMEN ON THE JOB

Few auto mechanics are women. In 2022, women made up about 12 percent of auto service mechanics. Women are generally not encouraged to apply for most trade jobs. If they apply, they may face employers who doubt their ability to do the job. And women who do find work as auto mechanics are generally paid less than men.

But these issues don't stop some women from becoming successful auto mechanics. Patrice Banks never felt comfortable bringing her car to auto shops with no female mechanics. So, she decided to become an auto mechanic herself. In 2016, she started her own auto repair shop in Upper Darby, Pennsylvania. Her shop

Women with an interest in cars who like to solve problems and work with their hands are good candidates for auto mechanic positions.

is unique because all the mechanics working there are women. She wanted women to feel comfortable bringing their cars to her. She said, "People are coming in, especially women, with that guard up. In order to get them to trust you, you have to let that guard down."[8] Banks proved that women can be auto mechanics, too.

A CAREER PEOPLE COUNT ON

There are a lot of reasons to become an auto mechanic. It is a great career for people who like cars. People who like to work with their hands might consider the career as well. Those who enjoy solving problems may also like fixing cars. A person interested in becoming an auto mechanic must decide how to train. They can become an apprentice. Or they can earn a vocational degree in automotive technology.

For many people in the United States, it's hard to imagine life without cars. As long as cars are in demand, auto mechanics will be in demand, too. Those who decide to become auto mechanics can look forward to a career with a bright future filled with opportunities for advancement.

GLOSSARY

air filter

a part in a car that cleans the air entering the engine

diagnostic

meant to discover the cause of a problem

fuel efficient

designed to use the least amount of fuel to travel the farthest distance

hydraulics

devices that use liquid pressure to exert force

industry

a group of businesses that make similar products or offer similar services

shadow

to spend a day with someone to learn about their job

solvents

chemicals that dissolve other substances

vocational colleges

post-secondary schools where students receive training for specific careers

SOURCE NOTES

INTRODUCTION: WHY BECOME AN AUTO MECHANIC?

1. Quoted in "A Day in the Life of an Auto Technician," *YouTube*, uploaded by OCADA, June 2, 2017. www.youtube.com.

CHAPTER ONE: WHAT DOES AN AUTO MECHANIC DO?

2. Dustin Peugeot, "Automotive Mechanic Skills Required by Employers," *Matrix Trade Institute*, February 6, 2019. www.matrixtradeinstitute.com.

CHAPTER TWO: WHAT TRAINING DO AUTO MECHANICS NEED?

3. Quoted in Brendan LaChance, "PHOTOS: NCHS Student Spends Final Days as a Senior Helping Repair School Buses During Two-Week Job Shadow," *Oil City News*, June 23, 2021. www.oilcity.news.

4. Quoted in "Interview with an Auto Mechanic—Q&A," *Auto Mechanic School Edu*, n.d. www.automechanicschooledu.org.

CHAPTER THREE: WHAT IS LIFE LIKE AS AN AUTO MECHANIC?

5. Quoted in "Diesel Mechanic Becomes Instructor: 'Now It's My Turn to Give Back,'" *SkillPointe*, February 26, 2021. www.skillpointe.com.

6. Faye Hadley, "My Five Favorite Things About Working on Cars," *Brenton Productions*, May 18, 2021. www.brentontv.com.

CHAPTER FOUR: WHAT IS THE FUTURE FOR AUTO MECHANICS?

7. Quoted in "Student Spotlight: Jeremy Ross Jr., Class of 2020," *Car Tracks*, Spring 2020. www.yatc.org.

8. Quoted in Terry Gross, "Girls Auto Clinic Owner: 'I Couldn't Find a Female Mechanic, So I Had to Learn,'" *NPR*, January 9, 2018. www.npr.org.

FOR FURTHER RESEARCH

BOOKS

Mike Downs, *Become an Aircraft Mechanic*. San Diego, CA: BrightPoint Press, 2025.

Gary Sprott, *Mechanics*. Greensboro, NC: Rourke Educational Media, 2020.

Sophie Washburne, *Great Car Designs*. New York: Cavendish Square Publishing, 2023.

INTERNET SOURCES

"How to Become a Mechanic," *Become*, March 9, 2023. www.learnhowtobecome.org.

Lurah Lowery, "Future Technology: What Shops Likely Will See Soon and by 2035," *Repairer Driven News*, February 22, 2022. www.repairerdrivennews.com.

"Why You Should Consider a Career in the Skilled Trades," *Lower Columbia College*, August 6, 2021. www.lowercolumbia.edu.

WEBSITES

ApprenticeshipUSA
www.apprenticeship.gov

ApprenticeshipUSA is an official US government website that connects those seeking apprenticeships with shops and mechanics that offer them.

International Automotive Technicians Network
www.iatn.net

The International Automotive Technicians Network connects more than 80,000 auto mechanics from around the world. Members share technical knowledge and discuss industry news.

National Institute for Automotive Service Excellence
www.ase.com

The National Institute for Automotive Service Excellence offers certifications in automotive technology. Information about the different options available can be found on its website.

INDEX

Cover: © Ground Picture/Shutterstock Images
5: © Roman Chazov/Shutterstock Images
7: © Taras.Chaban/Shutterstock Images
8: © Svitlana Hulko/Shutterstock Images
10: © Sudheer Sakthan/Shutterstock Images
13: © Egor Tetiushev/Shutterstock Images
15: © Poppy Pix/Shutterstock Images
16: © Eric Glenn/Shutterstock Images
19: © tigercat_lpg/Shutterstock Images
21: © madtufmr/Shutterstock Images
23: © runzelkorn/Shutterstock Images
24: © Matis75/Shutterstock Images
27: © Monkey Business Images/Shutterstock Images
28: © Stoyan Yotov/Shutterstock Images
31: © Monkey Business Images/Shutterstock Images
32: © Roman Chazov/Shutterstock Images
35: © Feeling Lucky/Shutterstock Images
37: © Potashev Aleksandr/Shutterstock Images
38: © Varavin88/Shutterstock Images
41: © H_Sutthichai/Shutterstock Images
43: © Photology1971/Shutterstock Images
44: © zedspider/Shutterstock Images
47: © LightField Studios/Shutterstock Images
51: © Ground Picture/Shutterstock Images
52: © Roman Zaiets/Shutterstock Images
54: © goodluz/Shutterstock Images
56: © Monkey Business Images/Shutterstock Images

Ib Larsen is a writer and editorial assistant living in Saint Paul, Minnesota.